The Anchored Soul

DEBORAH LYNNE

authorHOUSE®

AuthorHouse™
1663 Liberty Drive
Bloomington, IN 47403
www.authorhouse.com
Phone: 1-800-839-8640

First published by AuthorHouse 4/19/2011

ISBN: 978-1-4567-5824-0 (e)
ISBN: 978-1-4567-5825-7 (sc)

Printed in the United States of America

Thanks to friends, family, and acquaintances, who knowingly, and unknowingly, assisted, suggested or supported me throughout this project. To my niece Layla, I love you. "Whosoever shall humble himself as this little child, the same is greatest in the kingdom of heaven" (Matthew 18:4).

Acknowledgement

"For I neither received it of man, neither was I
taught it, but by the revelation of Jesus Christ"
(Galatians 1:12)

Introduction

The Anchored Soul is a 30 day devotional designed to lay a sure foundation to build upon. I highly recommend that it be read as such. You may even decide to re-read and meditate on any given day, yet continue to read in sequence, once you are ready to move on. Therefore it may take some longer than 30 days to read. When you chose to read the Anchored Soul, you chose to allow the Lord to speak to you, and in his timing. "But beloved, be not ignorant of this one thing, that one day is with the Lord as a thousand years, and a thousand years as one day" (2nd Peter 3:8).

A Call to Feast

After about one month of praying, fasting, worshipping, reading my bible, and listening to gospel music, I thought to myself "I need balance". All of my time was being spent on the things of the Lord. I had experienced a season similar to this some years ago. I allowed the enemy to get a foot hold, and plant the thought in my mind that I was bored living a Christian life. Eventually backsliding.

Now as I look back, I see that I was practicing devotional things, but not living a devoted life. Deceiving myself, therefore the enemy did likewise and deceived me. Well he was only doing what comes natural for him.

At this time I am devoted to God, and that brings about spiritual maturity. That maturity is developed over a period of time for some, and for others it may develop quickly, depending on the individual desire. In this season I am doing the same things I had did years earlier, and I hear the Lord saying " it is necessary". While meditating on those words, I saw myself in a place where I did not feel like getting on my knees to pray, or lifting my hands in praise, with no desire to fast, and quickly reading one verse in my bible and closing it even quicker. At this point I visualized a reserve tank (a storing place for future use)

"Cast thy bread upon the waters: for thou shalt find it after many days". (Ecclesiastes 11:1). Being that our daily bread is the Word of God (Matthew 4:4), and in our bellies is living water, after digesting the Word after many days we can draw from our reserve tanks in times of famine. They do and will come.

"In the morning sow thy seed, and in the evening withhold not thine hand: for thou knowest not whether shall prosper, either this or that, or whether they both shall be alike good". In reading that we can confidently say something will occur, it will prosper and it will be good. We are in a win/win situation here. So lets sow our seed, which is the Word of God (Matt.13:18-23) and not withhold our hands but lift them up in praise (1Tim. 2:8), then we can expect prosperity and goodness to be apart of our lives.

Day 1

Today's Challenge

Set aside 24 minutes, to spend with the Lord. In doing so you are tithing your time. If you find it hard to do, keep account of the time you spend with the Lord throughout the day, making sure it adds up to 24 minutes. For those who already spend that much time or more take a couple of minutes to pray for me (lol).

"Notes"

Contentment

Do you feel your home is too small? Are you unhappy at your current place of employment? Are you discontent in other areas of your life? Do you want to do something about it? How about learning to be in a state of contentment just where you are. "Not that I speak in respect of want; for I have learned, in whatsoever state I am, therewith to be content". (Philippians 4:11). As children of God to feel otherwise is not pleasing unto the Lord.

Although to desire prosperity is biblical, it is not the reward in itself. It is a fringe benefit we have as children of God. The actual reward we should be seeking is the Kingdom of God and all the fringe benefits will be added. "Beloved, I wish above all things that thou mayest prosper and be in health, even as thy soul prospers" (3rd John 1:2). There is no doubt that our soul will prosper (the Kingdom of God), and then we get benefits. What a glorious thing to be a child of the King.

"His lord said unto him, well done, good and faithful servant; thou hast been faithful over a few things, I will make thee ruler over many; enter thou into the joy of thy lord". (Matt. 25;23).

Take care of that 10 year- old car; fix up the one-bedroom apartment. And by all means minister to the two or three people God puts in your path, and watch your ministry grow. Godliness with contentment is great gain. Finally, to live in a state of discontentment can be likened to damnation. "Hell and destruction are never full; so the eyes of man are never satisfied" (Proverbs 27:20).

Today's Challenge

Leave home with extra cash in your wallet, just for the sake of having it. Tomorrow after gas allowance, and lunch, leave home with $1.00, monitor your thoughts, attitudes and actions.

"Notes"

Oh no, I'm losing my mind

After being hospitalized for what appeared to be a nervous breakdown, I called my sister, and as I was relating the episode to her I blurted out "the devil took my mind, and that is the best thing that could of ever happened" (I was in need of some serious renewing). My sister really got a laugh out of that. Afterwards I realized just how profound that statement was.

By no means are we to allow the enemy to take control of our minds. However our minds are to be renewed. "And be not conformed to this world: but be ye transformed by the renewing of your mind that ye may prove what is that good, and acceptable, and perfect will of God." (Romans 12:2).

After that step to continually, constantly, and consistently submit to God's will. Submit is: to let, to allow. "Let this mind be in you which was also in Christ Jesus".

If you have ever paid a visit to a mental facility, you know it is alarming how many of the patients quote the bible or babble on and on about spiritual matters. One of the reasons for these occurrences, is that during the transformation process, some try to compromise and negotiate which parts of their mind they will allow to be transformed and which parts they desire to hold on to. "Therefore to him who knows to good and does it not, to him it is sin". (James 4:17).

When the Holy Spirit leads us one way and we choose another, it is sin. After that comes the danger zone. "And even as they did not like to retain God in their knowledge, God gave them over to a reprobate mind, to do those things which are not convenient". (Romans1:28).

One of the definitions for reprobate is: a person beyond hope of salvation. Now that is losing your mind. Let us be sensitive and obedient to the Holy Spirit

Today's Challenge

Choose four hour intervals during the course of the day, set your alarm, (we do have them on our cell phones). Each time the alarm goes off, think on theses things, whatsoever things are honest, just, pure, lovely, of a good report of any virtue or praise. (Philippians 4:8)

"Notes"

Being A Friend of God's

I marveled the first time I heard someone speak about their friendship with God. I always knew Him to be a friend to the friendless. But the word friendship implies that both parties are actively involved, it is a joint venture/effort.

In listening to this young lady I heard a genuine intimacy. I began thinking to myself "God loves her more than he loves me". God knows our every thought, and He replied; " no, that is not true, however what is true is that she loves me more than you do"! (ouch). I will admit that I was lacking in many, many areas of my spiritual life. I immediately felt a sadness come over me. There has to be something I can do about this dilemma, and the answer is in The Book.

"Draw near to God and He will draw near to you. Cleanse your hands you sinners, and purify your hearts you double minded." (James 4:8).

Well it did not get any clearer than that, But I needed more, so I took out my concordance (GET ONE) and it led me to my next step.

"And the scripture was fulfilled which says Abraham BELIEVED GOD, and it was accounted to him for righteousness. And he was called the FRIEND OF GOD". (James 2:23).

At this point I was seeing, specifications and requirements that were necessary to obtain this "friendship". And as we grow spiritually I have no doubt, the requirements will increase in order to maintain that certain level of intimacy we so desire, remember to whom much is given much is required.

"A friend loves at all times, and a brother is born for adversity" (Proverbs 17:17).

Today's Challenge

When a friend or family member phones you tell them you will return the call shortly. And take that time to talk to the Lord instead. I am not referring to petitioning prayer. Tell him how your day is going, and what he means to you. He enjoys hearing from us, it brings Him joy. Imagine us bringing the Lord joy. We can and we do!

"Notes"

Day 5

Praying for the Salvation of Others

We so often become discouraged in this area of our prayer life. I know with a certainty that my grandmother prayed for me until her death. Yet it was still many years after her death, that I truly surrendered my life to the Lord Jesus. We are instructed to always pray and not faint (Luke 18:1).

Let's begin with scripture and continue there, we should desire to do things according to God's will and God's way. That can always be found in His word.

"And he said, hearken ye, all Judah, and ye inhabitants of Jerusalem, and thou King Jehoshaphat "Thus says the Lord unto you, Be not afraid nor dismayed by reason of this great multitude; for the battle is not yours but the Lord's"(2 Chronicles 20:15)

There is a battle going on and the main objective is souls. The enemy is after souls and he is playing for keeps. Remember that this is just another battle in the overall war. And the good news is that we who are in Christ Jesus have won. Yes the results are already in!

"No man can come to me, except the Father which sent me draw him: and I will raise him up at the last day" (John 6:44).

In directing our prayer according to that scripture, we focus on the mighty, saving power of God and not on the power of man. We also develop a compassion for others as we remember how, we were also once lost in our sins until The Lord drew us, there was nothing we could of done in and of ourselves.

"Or do you despise the riches of His goodness, forebearance and long suffering, not knowing that the goodness of God leads to repentance" (Romans 2:4).

The goodness of God can and does lead to repentance, however that is not to say that some will not have a Jonah or Saul/Paul experience. We can not limit God and how He chooses to bring about deliverance and salvation to fulfill His divine plan. We can rest assured that all things work together for the good to them that love the Lord and called according to His purpose.

Daily Prayer

Dear Lord,

Please send your servants on a holy mission concerning --------------, Lord place godly people in their paths, that everywhere the soles of their feet go, may someone say, "God bless you", another say "Jesus loves you", while yet another says "God is good". Lord your word says you are not slack concerning your promises, as some men count slackness; but is longsuffering to us-ward that any should perish, but that all should come to repentance". Amen.

Love is A Motivator

I gave my life to Jesus Christ at an early age. It seemed the most natural thing to do being that I was in the company of godly people the majority of the time. Besides my relatives there was also the "saints". Back in those days, the saints not only attended church on Sundays but they also fellowshipped during the week at each others homes. Even with this foundation, I still backslid as a teenager, and went out into the world to "do my thing". I did everything I could possibly do, and even those things I could not do, those are the things that would lead to me being incarcerated.

On this particular stay in jail, I felt worse than I had ever felt in my entire life. I was depressed, disgusted with myself, and physically ill on top of all that. As I lay in my bunk, I heard myself repeating the name of Jesus over and over. That in itself is not unusual, people automatically call on the name of Jesus when in trouble or pain. But this time I paused and remembered that Jesus was not just a name to me. It was the name of my savior. And if ever I needed a savior, it was at that moment. I knew right then that I had to confess my sins.

"If we confess our sins. He is faithful and just to forgive

us our sins and to cleanse us from all unrighteousness (1 John 1:9).

I began serving the Lord. Initially my circumstances was the motivating force that caused me to call on the name of Jesus. All was going well until I had a stirring in my soul. I was no longer focusing on my physical and natural state, I became concerned about my soul. I did not want to go to hell. With that in mind I grew even closer to the Lord. So at this point I see my desire to go to heaven and escape hell had motivated me to another level in my spiritual walk. Now here I am healed, saved and on my way to heaven. End of story? No. The Word of God was yet alive within me, and had no plans of returning void.

"You shall LOVE THE Lord your God with all your. And with all your mind". (Matthew 22:37).

I had fallen in love with the Lord. I periodically check my motives for serving the Lord, it is a habit I have acquired over time. I am going to be brutally honest here. There are many motives and reasons that people have for serving the Lord. Material gain, a good marriage, safety and protection are just to name a few. For us we are to recognize those things as just a few of the many benefits that are comes along with serving the Lord.

"Bless the Lord O my soul and forget not all his benefits" (Psalms 103:2). Our goal should be to make Love the Motivator, at the end of the day.

Today's Challenge

It is easy to love our family and friends, the true test is loving the unlovely. Ask the Lord to show you something you can do for someone where love is not automatically there. Feeding the homeless, sending someone a five dollar give card and not signing your name, or even a simple phone call. the key here is to then forget about what you did, as if it was the most natural thing to do, because it was the right thing to do (LOVE).

The "p" Word

After we begin to experience God and receive revelation, knowledge, and wisdom, there will come a time when we must deal with pride. As growing Christians we are to confront this issue when and as often as it may arise. This can be often, being we are transformed from glory to glory.

"But we all, with unveiled face beholding as in a glass the glory of the Lord, are changed into the same image from glory to glory, even as by the Spirit of the Lord".

Therefore we are to pray even more so, that we be led by the Spirit. Flesh is very prideful, and no flesh shall glory in his presence. I fell victim to the sin of pride. I recently had to be chastised once again in that area.

I had done something that I knew was not pleasing unto the Lord. I immediately asked for forgiveness. However I continued to feel condemned. No, I did not commit a capital offence, but judging from my reaction, one would assume I had. It was actually a small matter but nevertheless sin is sin in the sight of God. Throughout the day I began to hear the word pride drop into my spirit. I tried ignoring it. But once you know that still small voice there is no denying it. I had just sinned. Where does pride fit into this picture? The problem did not lie with the sin itself, but in how I reacted to the sin. See provisions have been made for us when we fall short.

"For I delivered to you first of all that which I also received, how that Christ died for our sins".

"There is therefore now no condemnation to those who are in Christ Jesus, who walk not after the flesh, but after the Spirit". (Romans 8:1).

Condemnation is not of God. Thinking we are above sin is fleshly pride, and the enemy will deceive us into thinking it is spiritual pride. There is nothing godly about pride. If it is spiritual pride one would be wise to question what spirit is influencing them. Remember Satan majored in pride, which was ultimately his downfall. If you feel you are a victim of spiritual pride, you can always test the spirit by the spirit. If in any doubt Galatians 5:13 gives a list of the fruits of the spirit. In studying the Word we will get an understanding as to what is sin, and how we are not to "practice" it. The entire book of 1st John is very enlightening on this subject matter.

And finally I once read that true wisdom, is knowing there is so much more to learn.

Today's Challenge

Give yourself a humbling experience. Do something you would never do in and of yourself. Instead of walking over that piece of paper on the ground, bend over and pick it up and while you are down there thank the Lord for the activity of your limbs. There are many things we can do. If we humble ourselves it prevents God from doing it, and we do not want that. Read about King Nebuchadnezzars humbling experience in the book of Daniel chapter 4.

Day 8

Let's Talk About Tithing

One of my most blessed experiences was in tithing. And it was not a financial blessing. While on vacation in Southern California, I attended Wednesday night bible study at a pretty big congregation. They were in the process of expanding the facility, and had been for quite some time. I knew this because I had attended services there on previous occasions. Each time funds for the expansion seemed to be the focal point. And to no surprise of mine we were asked to turn to the book of Malachi. I left there that night discouraged, I was seeking a Word from the Lord (and oh boy, I eventually received one).

The following Saturday I was still in Southern California, and God spoke to me in that still small, undeniable voice. Next thing I knew I was at the ATM withdrawing money to pay tithes, and was to pay them at the very church that I had left feeling so discouraged.. I obeyed. We are told in the Word to be cheerful givers, but I had not yet arrived.

Due to the size of the congregation there are three services held on Sundays. I attended the 11:00 service, and did as the Lord had instructed me to do. At the end of service the Pastor asked those in need of prayer to stand. I can never have too much prayer, so I stood. At that point my friend says to me "He only mean those who are not saved". I continued to stand, and we all raised our hands in prayer. The pastor then made an altar call for those who so desired, to come. It was then that I decided to take my seat. The Pastor pointed in the general area where I was seated, and says "someone right in there needs to come down". I knew in my spirit that it was ME. Oh no, he knows about my issue with paying tithes into this ministry (let me stress here, that the Lord does indeed bless obedience). As the pastor begins to pray he looks directly at me and I shift my eyes downward, he says "You, look at me" then he began to prophesy life to my spirit. I can not quote the exact words, but they went something like this. "The Lord wants you to know, he sees your desire to serve him, he knows your heart and knows all you have been through and Satan desires to sift you as wheat, because you are a powerful woman of God." I looked around and saw the whole congregation rejoicing. I later found out that was only one of a very few times they had heard their pastor prophesy. On occasion he would have prophets come to a special service and deliver a prophetic word. We see here that God can and does use anyone he choose, in any area he choose, and at any time he chooses. The key is to be a yielded, and willing vessel fit for the Masters use. That is when we can say as the prophet Isaiah said "here am I, send me" (Isaiah 6:8)

Today's Challenge

Pay your tithes.

Day 9

Developing a Genuine Thirst for the Lord and Having it Quenched

"But he answered and said, it is written, Man shall not live by bread alone, but by every word that proceedeth out of the mouth of God" (Matt. 4:4).

"Give us this day our daily bread". (Matt. 6:11).

In the spiritual we know that our daily bread is the Word of God. In both of these scriptures we find ourselves eating spiritually. In the natural sense, after eating we get thirsty. Do you not know this applies in the spiritual as well? And from personal experience I would say even more so. The Word of God is how we develop this thirst. Then the Lord himself quenches that thirst. He truly is an all sufficient God. Today we will just read over some scripture to see just how important it is to develop that thirst and have it quenched as well. First and foremost it is a blessing.

"Blessed are those who hunger and thirst for righteousness, for they shall be filled" (Matt. 5:6).

But whosoever drinketh of the water that I shall give him shall never thirst; but the water I shall give shall be in him a well of water springing up into everlasting life" (John 4:14).

"And Jesus said unto them, I am the bread of life; he that cometh to me shall never hunger, and he that believeth on me shall never thirst" (John 6:35.

If anyone thirst, let him come and drink" (John 7:37).

Jesus came to reconcile the world back to the Father, he desires us to come to him, he desires our thirst for him, it draws us to him. Since we get thirsty after eating, I would say we have some reading to do and some hearing to do as well. Lets be doers of the Word.

Today's Challenge

After reading a scripture today (your meal). Sit quietly for a moment, and you will develop what I call a thirst. Then the Lord will bring scriptures to mind that you have read previously, and they will confirm the scripture that you read and meditated on today, that is what I refer to as quenching your thirst (fulfilling). The key to this challenge is to pray, have faith, and expect, the Lord to feed you through His word and quench your thirst through His Spirit.

The Light, the Glory, and the Holy Spirit

"This little light of mine I'm going to let it shine".

"Jesus is the light of the world".

"And if I be lifted up from the earth, I will draw all men unto me" (John 12:32).

I have quoted a few of the words from songs I used to sing as a child. Whenever I think about light Jesus comes to mind. He is the light and in him is no darkness. When we become children of God we have that light (Jesus). Our desire should be that we let it shine so that people are enlightened about Jesus. As Christians often times we do just that unbeknownst to us. Now keep that in mind as move on to the Glory.

"Then a cloud covered the tent of the congregation, and the glory of the Lord filled the tabernacle" (Exodus 40:34).

As we read about the tabernacle and the glory of the Lord being there continuously, we also see that not just anyone could go into the tabernacle. There were requirements and specifications, as to whom could enter and how they were to enter. If they were not met, death occurred. There was nothing hidden once you came into the very presence of God (The Glory).

Even today when I experience the presence of God during worship, a death occurs. Some part of flesh dies, at times the Lord will reveal a sin or secret fault I have, and at other times I just feel lighter in my spirit. The Glory exposes sin and it is dealt with, again it can occur unbeknownst to us, (we will never truly know all of God's ways). Once we become children of God we too have the Glory of God upon us, just as Moses did.

"And when Moses saw that the people were naked;(for Aaron had made them naked unto their shame amongst their enemy)". (Exodus 26:30)

Although it is not mentioned in the text, I feel even if the Israelites had of attempted to hide themselves from Moses, it would have been to no avail, just as Adam and Eve did, in the Garden of Eden. Moses had been in the presence of God, and The Glory would of exposed them.

"For the Lord had said unto Moses, Say unto the children of Israel, ye are a stiffnecked people; I will come into the midst of thee in a moment, and consume thee; therefore now put off thy ornaments from thee, that I may know what to do with thee". And the children of Israel stript themselves of their ornaments by the mount Horeb" (Exodus 33:5-6).

Here we see God giving the Israelites the opportunity

to uncover them selves, and they did so because they knew exposure would occur. The same is true for us today. The Lord gives us the opportunity to confess our sins. If you have followed the exposure of some of today's popular leaders, that have fell from grace, you see that exposure is not a pretty sight. Confession is good for the soul.

Now being spirit filled children of God we have the ability to lead others to Christ (The Light) With the Glory we also have the ability to expose the enemy. How do we distinguish the difference, and when are we to use one or the other? WE DON'T! That is the work of the Holy Spirit.

"Howbeit when he, the Spirit of truth is come, he will guide you into all truths; for he shall not speak of himself, but whatsoever he shall hear that shall he speak, and he will shew you things to come". (John 16:13)

Not by any means am I implying that this is the sole purpose of The Light, The Glory, and The Holy Spirit. These are only some of the many ways that The Three work together as One.

Today's Challenges

1) Purpose in your heart to let your light shine today. give someone the right away in traffic, or any human act of kindness.

2) Spend some time in the presence of the Lord and ask Him to reveal a secret sin or fault (we all have them) it may not be evident immediately, but wait and be receptive.

3) Before going to sleep let the Holy Spirit minister to you. Listen, listen, listen. He does and will speak.

(None of these daily challenges are limited to the particular day that it is read. These challenges can and should be incorporated in our walk when and as often as needed).

God Will Restore

The majority of us have had things taken from us. And would like them restored. God is able to restore each and everything that Satan has attempted to take possession of. Yes, I did say attempt, because once it is restored, that means the siege was unsuccessful.

In Webster's dictionary one definition for restore is; to bring back into existence. So at some point "it" ceased to exist. And that being the time of the attempted siege. What God has for you is for you, and is of no use to anyone else.

Now we will look at another type of restoration, which is restoration of self. This is the restoration spoken of in the book of Joel, when the Lord speaks of restoring years, not material possessions.

"And I will restore to you the years that the locust hath eaten, the cankerworm, and the caterpillar, and the palmerworm, and my great army which I sent among you". (Joel 2:25). These different types of locusts and such are the same as the plagues God sent to Pharaoh, due to disobedience to His word. I so often hear people complain that the enemy took this or that, personally I feel at times he is given too much credit. His power is actually limited.

Another definition for restore, which is also in Webster's is: to bring back to a more desirable condition. This is the type that best describes one's condition before coming to Christ. I have witnessed drug and alcohol abusers being ostracized from their family, due to dishonesty, stealing etc. Children dis-owning one or the other parents due to past child abuse issues. I have also witnessed these same people giving their lives to Christ, and allowing him to make them new creatures. With the end result being, they actually became desirable, considered a joy to be around. You may not of went to any of the extremes that I mentioned above, but sin in itself makes us undesirable. I even look back over my life and see where I was un desirable in my own eyes. Recently I ran into a young lady that I was acquainted with during that time, to put it lightly we disliked each other. She approached me and asked that I pray for her. She did not even acknowledge that we had differences, she did not feel the least bit uncomfortable requesting prayer. "He leads me in the path of righteousness for His name's sake". She saw a change and knew it was God. He received the glory. that should be our desire at all times.

Today's Challenge

1) Think of something that has not been restored to you. maybe a relationship. Now thank the Lord, because it was not a good thing. He will not withhold no "good thing". (Psalms 84:11).

2) If you are waiting for something you are sure is a "good thing" start thanking the Lord for his perfect timing in your life, and consider it done.

Left Speechless

A couple of years ago I had the privilege of attending my first Women's Retreat. Ladies, gentlemen, couples, singles, and youth I strongly encourage you to make a spiritual retreat one of your annual to-do events.

I gave my life to Christ at an early age. His mercy, grace, love and forgiveness are a few of the many things I experienced. His very presence is now included on that list. It is undeniable and unexplainable. It varies with each individual. God is God, yet He is unique to each of us, because we are each unique to Him.

We were enjoying a worship session at the retreat. I have felt the Spirit of God in church, prayer meetings, and even alone while listening to music. But, this time I a personal visitation, the first of many more to come. It was as if there was no one in the room but me and Him. I was well aware of the other women, as they were praising, singing, crying, and some even laughing. Then I realized I was completely silent. I tried to say, halleluia, praise the Lord, thank you Jesus, or something, the words failed to come forth.

"But the Lord is in his holy temple: let all the earth keep silent before him". (Habakkuk 2:20).

As I finally accepted this newfound silence, the Lord began to minister to me. "It is impossible for you to express the praise you are experiencing. The thanks that you have for my mercy, grace, goodness and faithfulness is beyond human measure. If it were possible for you to express those things right now, you would never again close your mouth.". He truly knows us better than we know our selves that was precisely what I was feeling. "WHEW".

"A time to rent, and a time to sew: a time to keep silent, and a time to speak" (Ecclesiastes 3:7).

I have been speechless on a few occasions since then. I never know when I will experience it again, whenever that time is, it will be welcomed. Maybe that is why I prefer writing as opposed to public speaking, I laugh to myself as I visualize myself at a podium unable to speak.

Today's Challenge

Welcome silence for a while today, not necessarily expecting anything but the peace of God which surpasses all understanding.

The Lord's Employee

When the Holy Spirit led me to write on today's topic, I must admit I was a bit hesitant to say the least (I have never been the employee of the month). I was given one scripture to expound on. That was a change from the previous days, because the scriptures are what I use to edify, and confirm the word I receive from the Lord.

"With good will doing service, as to the Lord and not to men" (Ephesians 6:7).

In reading that verse, I knew the Lord would be speaking to the employed, self- employed, and unemployed as well. As I am striving to be an obedient servant I accepted the assignment. I have had numerous jobs, varying in time lengths. At the time I became disabled I will admit I did not have an impeccable work history to say the least. Nevertheless I stepped out on faith with pen in hand, I began writing from a personal viewpoint. I had no idea I even had a view on this subject. Little did I know I had became gainfully employed when I began writing "The Anchored Soul".

An application is basically personal information. I filled mine out when I confessed my sins. A resume is past experiences. That is my testimony. References are people that know you and something about you not just surface things. I have three; God the Father, Jesus Christ and the Holy Spirit. I have full benefits and my salary is negotiable.

In the beginning days of Anchored Soul, I worked whenever I felt like it. If it was early morning I stayed in my p.j's, and took random breaks. Now that I know this is my job, I have work hours and designated breaks. I no longer take advantage of my employer or my position. Can any one relate? Being presentable and punctual are first and foremost.

Next I tackled the issue of overtime. One day I wanted to work more than the hours I had decided upon. However, the words refused to flow, and that really bothered me because it was a first (although it does happen from time to time). As I prayed for an answer, the Lord showed me where other things would go neglected if I continued to write that day. I was not tired, I had put out a quality and a quantity of work that was acceptable. Why over work myself? If we find ourselves neglecting family, or other important obligations, losing sleep, being tired and irritable after working over time, it is time to take a look at things. And it may not be wise to work overtime. Those extra $$ can and do help, and are even absolutely necessary at times, but do use wisdom.

Calling in sick when you are not sick is lying. There is a difference in calling in sick and taking a sick day. I realize that circumstances and situations do arise, but as Christians lets try to maintain a certain level of integrity. I have touched on a few issues, however we all know are job descriptions and requirements upon being hired. Again, integrity.

"And he said unto them, how is it that ye sought me? wist ye not that I must be about my Father's business?" (Luke 2:49).

To the self-employed and business owners: The earth is the Lord's and the fullness thereof. We are stewards. Again integrity, i.e. cutting expenses, which causes quality service not to be rendered, and using unnecessary expenses to show off (meaning to go way over board, signals pride) fall into this category. Can any one relate? I have never owned a business, so, he who has an ear let him hear what says the Spirit of the Lord. Our desire should be to get it right, whatever it may be. In just taking heed to the obvious, will cause businesses to flourish. After we prove to be faithful over a few He will make us master over much.

And by the way, I now work in p.j.'s, that is one of the fringe benefits of being self-employed. We all know the benefits come into effect after a period of time. Business owners and the self-employed let's not take advantage of the favor God has showed us.

Today's Challenge

Volunteer for, whatever, whenever, wherever or who ever just do it. And do it as unto the Lord.

Satan Needs Permission

I mentioned this before, and I still believe that we give Satan too much credit. It is not due him. Satan had to ask permission to harass Job. I use the word harass, because the definition of harass is: to trouble by repeated attacks.

"And the Lord said unto Satan, Behold all that he hath is in thy power; only upon himself put not forth thine hand. So Satan went forth from the presence of the Lord" (Job 2:6).

We see not only does the Lord give Satan permission, he also determines to what extent Satan can go.

"And the Lord said unto Satan, Behold he is in thine hand; but save his life" (Job 2:6).

Again we see Satan has limitations, he comes back for futher permission. He could not just run rampant in Job's life, I'm sure he would have if he could have. God is the same yesterday, today, and forever. Just as in the case with Job, it is the same today. Satan needs permission.

"Verily, verily I say unto you, He that believeth on me, the works I do he do also, and even greater than these shall he do, because I go unto my Father" (John 14:12).

After Jesus went to the Father, the Holy Spirit was sent

to us to enable us to do those works. Now we have the authority to give Satan permission, and the power to limit him. The way we give the enemy permission is by opening the door to sin, and being disobedient unto the Lord. Satan can not just come into our lives and wreck havoc, with-out us opening a door, with the exception of being in a position such as Job was. Where as God knows how strong we are, and that we will not waiver in our spiritual walk, saying: for I know my redeemer lives. When we find ourselves under constant attack, we should ask ourselves two questions. 1) Am I strong enough in the Lord, that he would consider me able to endure this attack? 2) Or have I allowed sin to enter? Deep soul searching may be required. We sometimes have hidden sins and faults that the Lord will reveal, when we sincerely desire him to do so out of a pure heart.

Today's Challenge

Let's ask the Lord to reveal any hidden sin, or secret fault. Oftentimes they are things we struggled with previously, and never was delivered fully, the heart is deceitful, and the enemy is cunning. If nothing is revealed I strongly urge you to do this periodically. None of us have arrived. The apostle Paul says we die daily.

Difficult People

Before we start trying to figure out, and name difficult people, first ask ; am I one of those people? Second of all, if everyone you know is difficult, start within. Sometimes the Lord will allow a number of difficult people in your life all in the same season. This will occur usually before a great work he is going to perform through you, or while in the very midst of it, remember Moses and the children of Israel.

From my experiences the majority of difficult people are just plain angry. They have been for many years and have allowed that anger to fester and mold them into that "difficult person". They are everywhere, grocery stores, jobs, schools, DMV, and church, they will always be with us on this side of heaven. We must try to be prepared for when we are confronted with them, they also work in the perfecting of our faith, yes, truly all things work together for the good and that includes people as well.

"Make no friendship with an angry man and with a furious man do not go" (Proverbs 22:24).

Although we can not always avoid these people, yet we are not to form bonds with them. After the preliminaries, (hello and good-bye, how is the weather) you go your way and allow them to go theirs. Some will attempt to follow you, if that happens, lead them to Christ if at all possible, that is the only exception. Even in the event, which this appears to be the case, be wise, these are the days of great deception, ulterior motives, and hidden agendas.

In one of my experiences, this individual would try to attack me, using my spiritual walk! Not with harsh words, but with scripture i.e. "you have to forgive me seventy times seven", "the greatest commandment is love and you do not have it", and so on it would go. After a while the condemnation was more than I could bear. There is no condemnation for those who are in Christ Jesus (Romans 8:1). Take notice I did not quote the scriptures this individual was referring to, they were distorted and twisted with no life and no effectiveness. We all know otherwise, that the Word is alive and effective. I mention this incident, and relate it to Satan "trying" to use the Word. It is vital that we not only read, but also know our bibles.

There are some scriptures that ministered to me during this season. In the book of Genesis, we find Abraham and his nephew Lot traveling together, and strife arose among their herdsmen. Even though Abraham and Lot were blood relatives and the dispute was not between the two of them, yet they agreed to go separate ways to avoid strife (Genesis 13). No doubt we will have differences in opinion, and not always agree, however if there is constant strife that is not the will of God. Sometimes we have to actually weigh it out.

"The righteous choose his friends carefully, for the way of the wicked leads astray" (Proverbs 12:26). We are to love everyone; still we do have a choice as to their position in our life. Beware the enemy will try to flood you with guilt trips when he realizes he no longer has a position in your life. Because some people we do cut off completely.

"And if thy right hand offends thee, cut it off, and cast it from thee; for it is profitable for thee that one of thy members should perish, and not that thy whole body should be cast into hell" (Matthew 5:30).

After revelation of that scripture I immediately began to pray. I knew I would need wisdom, understanding and maturity to accept this; my right hand is a member of my body, just as I have family members, and church members. We can refer back to Abraham and Lot in cases such as these, and pray for the guidance of the Holy Spirit.

Ostracizing family members and leaving church is not always the answer, although it appears to be an easy way out (looks are deceiving). We are to be like Jesus, He prayed in the Garden of Gethsemane all night. He knew what was ahead for him, and that he would be betrayed, yet he prayed for strength. In dealing with difficult people God will give of strength. Through it all be joyful, the joy of the Lord is our strength.

Today's Challenge

Today we have an exercise, I hope you enjoy and utilize.

On a piece of paper draw a large circle. Within that circle will be circles. They can vary with the individual. In the center, you will place a dot. The outer circle represents mankind. The next circles will each represent neighbors and co-workers, followed by church folks, family, and confidants. When you get to the final circle it should only contain confidants, if I am correct there should be no more than one or two people within that circle. Now you will find your self in the center with the dot. The dot represents God. This should help in prioritizing, and balancing your associations.

Selfishness

At the beginning of today's reading, I am going to ask a simple question. Are you selfish. Guessing, I would say 85% of us would answer no. And believe it or not, after today's reading, if I were to pose the same question, 85% of us would answer yes. Amazing isn't it?

The enemy likes to whisper in our ears, and plant negative thoughts in our minds, most of which our untrue. How many times have you heard him say that you were selfish? If I am correct, it would be very few times if any. One reason being that Satan is the father of lies, and he would be speaking the truth.

There is an old saying, that self preservation is the first law of nature, I even quoted it before. I can agree with that, nature is speaking of natural things, however spiritually that is not so. Once we are spirit-filled we are not under natural laws, even though we live by some, we can still apply spiritual principals, which do not totally cancel out the natural order of things, but do over rule them. For example where same sex marriages are legal, (natural law) our spiritual principals over rule that law, even though it exists.

Back to the matter at hand (selfishness).

"Let nothing be done through strife or vainglory, but in lowliness of mind let each esteem others better than themselves. Look not every man on his own things, but every man also on the things of others" (Philippians 2:3-4).

"Be kindly affectioned one to another with brotherly love; in honor preferring one another" (Romans 12:10).

As Christians we do not want to be ignorant or turn a blind eye, when the Lord reveals ourselves to us. This will occur throughout our journey. Think it not strange the fiery trial that is to try you (dealing with self).

"Search me, O God and know my heart; try me and know my thoughts". (Psalms 139:23).

Some of us may still be answering, no to the question asked at the beginning. That's o.k . Just stay with me here. I was in denial too, until the Holy Spirit spoke to me and revealed the carnal aspect which is selfishness in itself.

Back in high-school some of us liked hanging out with attractive and popular people, even becoming romantically involved, and the person did not have to be nice. Why did we want to be around these people? For many of us, it was because they were pleasing to OUR eyes, or, because it made US feel important (self gratification). Many people will become sexually involved with someone, and because THEY are satisfied in that area, will take no consideration of the other area involved in order to make a relationship work. Sex outside of marriage is sin its called fornication.

A few years back I met a gentleman who desired to become intimate. I said NO not outside of marriage. His reply was; I need to test out how our sex life will be. Let 's get real here people, God who created everything, who knows us and our bodies better than we know ourselves, does not know how to bless a union and make every aspect of it "GREAT!!!!". Personally I prefer to wait and do it Gods way. He knows best and had our best interest in mind when he put laws, principle and commandments in order.

We all, or at least we should desire the Lord to come into our lives and our hearts. It is wonderful to have the Lord leading, guiding, protecting and blessing us. Can we take time out from these desires to seek what the Lord desires of us.

Why leap ye, ye high hills? this is the hill which God desireth to dwell in; yea, the Lord will dwell in it forever (Psalms 68:16).

In Exodus 35 and other scriptures as well, specific instructions are given in regards to the building and upkeep of the tabernacle, where the Lord was to dwell. Today we are the temple of the Living God. We have requirements that must be met in order to keep our temples clean. That means putting our selfish desires aside.

"And God blessed the seventh day, and sanctified it; because that in it he had rest from all his work which God created and made" (Genesis 2:3).

God blessed the Sabbath because he rested. So rest is good, God even enjoys it. Let us be that place where the Lord can rest, rule, dwell and abide, keep in mind He will not dwell in an unclean temple.

Today's Challenge

Ask not what more can the Lord do for me, but what can I
do for the Lord?

Driving an 18 Wheeler

I know you are wondering where in the world is this going. I'll get right to it. I have had this re-occurring dream for many years. In this dream I am driving this eighteen- wheeler big rig. I am so tired, but the only parking spaces will require me to parallel park this hugh thing, so I continue driving, end of dream. The obvious spiritual implication would be, to keep going on the straight and narrow way. However this dream has always left me with an uneasy feeling.

One morning after waking from one of these dreams, I prayed for revelation. I know after a revelation from God there is a peace, and I was not getting that peace by just taking this dream to mean the obvious. I love the way the Lord shows us things. In this dream what I needed was rest. Therefore it was imperative that I learn to park. Just imagine for a moment, having to parallel park a big truck, with absolutely no space left over. That is quite some maneuvering. Pull forward, back-up, cut the wheel just so, pull up just a tad, oops too much, and so on it goes. Liken that maneuvering to our spiritual walk.

"And he said unto them, Come ye yourselves apart into

a desert place, and rest a while; for there were many coming and going, and they had no leisure so much as to eat.

Using the eighteen-wheeler analogy, we will need rest after working through our, trials test, temptations, and tribulations. So rest up until the next time you have to park and get rest, it is detrimental.

Today's Challenge

Pick one thing you are facing today(preferable some thing small). Work your way through it, not stopping until you get an absolute peace about the situation. Then REST!!

What is Required?

I so often ask myself am I doing enough, am I fruitful? Do I show compassion? Do I show mercy? Like with all other questions the answer is in the Book.

"But he that knew not, and did not commit things worth of stripes, shall be with few stripes, for unto much is given, of him shall much be required; and to whom men have committed much, of him they will ask the more" (Luke 12:48).

When Jesus gave his life for us, I would definitely call that, giving each and every one of us much. So I ask again what is required of us? As defined in Webster's much is; a great in quantity, measure, or degree: a great notable thing or matter. I will sum it up as; a great measure of an important thing.

Everything God gives us is important, whether it be; spiritual, material(things), financial(money), or natural(self). We see here that "Much" can cover a wide range of things. And we are to give "Much". As with all other things we are to use wisdom in our giving, we are not to give to the point that we lack, unless we hear something specifically from

God and not man, in those cases God will provide. In the event He does not, it was not him. WISDOM.

Here is an example of how much can be given spiritually. During the altar call at a Sunday worship service, I remained in my seat, praying quietly for the people who had went up. Yet I still felt more was required of me. At this time I was in a season of much prayer and fasting, and consecration, if ever I could get a prayer straight to the throne, now was the time (at times we do feel a little more confident than at other times). My attention was drawn to one particular lady, who had been missing quite a few services. No, I do not monitor other member attendance, actually I am too busy getting all I can out of each service, but she is missed by everyone when she is out, due to the fact she sings the loudest, beats the tambourine and dance the most. As I sat there praying specifically for her and her needs whatever they were, she began praising the Lord, it was a new praise for her. There was no music, tambourine, or dancing. She was in worship such as never before. The anointing of God was evident without the hype. This is not to take any thing away from any form of worship, I love it all. That day I left feeling I had purpose, my prayers were effective, and much was required of me. Just quietly sitting in my seat proved that, we all can do much, and it's not to get credit from man but to give Gory to God.

Today's Challenge

Attend the bible study you do not usually attend, attend an evening service, anything outside of the bare minimal is considered much. Try It.

Am, I Merely Happy or do I Possess Genuine Joy?

Happiness occurs because of an event. It is a state of mind. It is temporal. Joy is in spite of any given situation, and regardless to the circumstances. It is eternal.

"Happy is that people, that is in such a case; yea, happy is that people whose God is the Lord" (Psalms 144:15).

Just because these people acknowledge God is Lord made them happy. It goes beyond acknowledgement to possess joy. Even the heathen acknowledge God. Take a look at our currency, (in God we trust). Money does have a tendency to bring happiness, but then what?

Do you merely acknowledge God? Or do you believe, trust, obey, and have salvation? Those are the factors that determine whether you are happy or have joy.

The joy of the Lord is our strength (Nehemiah 8:10). Another win/win situation. That is just how it is on the Lord's side

Today's Challenge

Think of a present unpleasant situation, and think about it until it makes you uneasy, an unhappy feeling. Now focus on all that God has done and all that He has promises. The level of joy surpasses the unhappiness, and even the happiness if the situation was resolved, if you just think: when all is said and done I am going to heaven. WHEW!!!!

Day 20

Let Jesus Be the Reason

Some of you may recall a gospel song entitled "We Fall Down but We Get Up". It was very popular, and truly a blessing to me. One day as, myself and others were listening to this song, I could not help but to stop and notice how everyone was really into singing along. At the time I was not serving the Lord, and to the best of my knowledge no one else there was either.

After giving my life back to the Lord, I remembered that particular afternoon clearly. It was dropped into my spirit so strongly, that I began to meditate, which I often do when this happens.

"For a just man falleth seven times, and riseth up again, but the wicked shall fall into mischief ". (Proverbs 24:16).

When reading the Bible, always know to whom the Lord is speaking to, and who he is speaking about. Often we are guilty of reading the Bible for self-gratification, rationalization and justification. That is not to say we are not justified, we are due to the finished work at Calvary. The question is: does that justification fit you and you current circumstances? We are not only to search the scriptures; research is required as well.

After my meditation, I could plainly see that those individuals, on that day, were using the words of that song as an excuse to continue in their sinful ways. As believers we are to have an entirely different views. We are to look at the reasons why we serve the Lord, and not for excuses to sin. Here is one of the many reasons that I serve the Lord: "For God so loved the world that he gave his only begotten Son, that whosoever believeth in him should not perish, but have everlasting life".

Now that is love. And because of it, we are now able to be forgiven and, in right standing with God when we fall short. Les us rejoice in the reason, and not wallow in the excuses.

Today's Challenge

Think of one of your favorite verses. Go to that verse and read the entire chapter, in some cases the entire book. Pray before doing this challenge, and expect the Holy Spirit to give you a new revelation.

"Notes"

Winning Our Daily Battles

We are in battle against the wicked and evil forces in this present world. For some, it is their ministry to engage in spiritual warfare. For others we are to fast, pray, read the Word, and spend quality time the Lord and in doing this, if and when the occasion calls for spiritual warfare we are prepared. I do not advise any of us to go around casting out demons and engaging in such things, unless God directs us to do so, even then absolute obedience is a must.

"Put on the whole armour of God, that ye may be able to stand against the wiles of the devil" (Ephesians 6:11).

This armour is God's and consists of his righteousness. This is not the "Sunday" only type of righteousness. Because of that type of righteousness (self-righteousness or unrighteousness) the enemy is able to infiltrate the church. He can not stand to be around the righteousness of God. He hates it, and he will flee.

"If ye abide in me and my words abide in you, ye shall ask what ye will, and it shall be dine unto you" (John 15:7).

"For the word of God is quick, and powerful, and sharper than any two-edged sword, piercing even to the dividing asunder of soul and spirit, and of the joint and marrow, and is a discerner of the thoughts and intents of the heart" (Hebrews 4:12).

With the word abiding in us, and the word being sharper than any two-edged sword, I am able to get a visual of us walking, going about our daily activities, and doing damage to any demonic force that comes within distance of us. AMEN.

Today's Challenge

Purpose in your heart to have a two-edged sword on your person today. Which simply means READ YOUR BIBLE and internalize it, hide it in your heart.

"Notes"

Who Do Men Say I Am?

As far back as I can remember I have always been a believer. No, it was not because I was saved or even wanted to be, it was because I went to church and was taught to believe that Jesus is the Christ, the Son of the Living God. Being to young to dispute, debate, or question, I automatically believed.

"He saith unto them, But whom say ye that I am?" (Matthew 16:15)

Today I not only believe that Jesus is who he says he is. I am persuaded, I claim him to be who he is. The Christ, The Son of God, My Savior, My Redeemer, The Lily of the Valley, The Bright and Morning Star, The Rose of Sharon, The King of Kings, The Alpha and Omega, My All in All.

"And Simon Peter answered and said, Thou art the Christ, the Son of the Living God"(Matthew 16:16). Do you know who Jesus is? Are you persuaded? Can you claim Him to be who he is, based on a personal experience? We all can come to that point beyond belief, and even further, depending on our desire to know him. The apostle Paul wrote "Oh to know him and the power of his resurrection".

"And Jesus answered, and said unto him, Blessed art thou Simon Barjona; for flesh and blood hath not revealed it unto thee, but my Father which is in heaven" (Matthew 16:17).

Today's Challenge

Think back to the first time you had a personal experience with Jesus, and Thank God for the revelation. If you can not remember, consider The Anchored Soul that encounter, you are not reading this book by accident.

Knowing God for Yourself

I had downloaded some praise and worship music on my mp3 player, and was enjoying every minute of it. I would begin with a song of worship to usher in the presence of the Lord, followed by a song of praise, then offer up thanksgiving. I had it all together, a routine you could say.

One morning I woke up and just stayed in bed praying, no music. As time moved on I realized I had not read my Bible, and had no desire to either. "Lord I do not understand this". My telephone was off. I normally would have touched bases with one of my two sisters for encouragement. Never-the-less I went on with my day, and surprisingly with no conviction from the Holy Spirit. What is this about?

That evening as I kneeled to pray, I heard these words come from my mouth: Lord thank you for allowing me to come to you on my own. Not always needing a pastor, for one day I may be unable to attend church. Not always needing music to usher me into your presence, for one day my hearing my grow dull. Not always needing my bible, for one day my eyes may fail me.

"Thy word have I hid in my heart, that I might not sin against thee" (Psalms119:11).

As long as we are in these earthen vessels, and our hearts beat we can experience the presence of God. Imagine having Alzheimer's disease, yet communing with the Lord in our hearts though the word he instructed us to hide there.

Can you reach the Lord? At any time? Any place? He is always there. Are you doing your part?

Today's Challenge

Memorize an encouraging scripture, I know some of us have memorized many. The next time you are in need of someone to talk to, or pray with you, and your bible is not in your hands at the moment, retrieve the word that you hid in your heart.

Feed My Sheep

As I was going about my daily activities, I heard this question: Do you love me? Some time later I again heard the same question. And it continued to be asked of me throughout the day. I recalled Jesus asking Peter the same question. However I had to turn to my bible for the exact context of that scripture.

"He saith unto him the third time, Simon son of Jonas, lovest thou me? Peter was grieved because he said unto the third time, Lovest thou me? And he said unto him, Lord thou knowest all things: thou knowest that I love thee. Jesus said unto him, Feed my sheep>" (John 21:17).

I began praying immediately. Lord, am I going to have a church? Well I need to know my sheep, so I can feed them. God being faithful, revealed my sheep to me, and to my great surprise I already had them.

My son was incarcerated at this time. About a month, before, he had mentioned a young man there, who had lost contact with his family and no one was writing him. I began corresponding with him. There was an old high school friend who had been incarcerated for quite some time, and I had started communicating with him. Who in turn knew someone that needed a friendly hello, and a few stamps to write home. Then there was the gentleman in another state, who had recently lost his mother, I was an acquaintance of his cousins, and she asked that I write him.

Here I was already in ministry and not even aware of it. I knew God was in control, because this was due to no effort on my behalf.

"And all things are of God, who hath reconciled us to himself by Jesus Christ, and hath given to us the ministry of reconciliation">. (2nd Corinthians 5:18).

Do you know your sheep? Are you feeding them? Are you tending to them? If you can not answer yes to these questions, you can always pray about it, so that you may become more effective. Above all, we are to live as Christians (like Christ) at all times, because we may never know all of the sheep God gives us, until we get our rewards in heaven. He can do exceedingly, above all we can ask or think.

Today's Challenge

Give someone a scripture to read today. whether they read it or not, it is an act of obedience, we are to spread the gospel. In these modern days there is texting, e-mail, facebook, you can even leave voice messages. Also you can order copies of the daily bread and randomly distribute them, although it would only be randomly on your behalf, our footsteps are ordered.

Becoming Childlike

"And said, Verily I say unto you, except ye be converted, and become as little children, ye shall not enter into the kingdom of heaven" (Matthew 18:3).

When I began writing this book it coincided with the time I began caring for Layla (my niece). She was eight months, and such a joy to watch. I get pleasure when I think of our heavenly Father enjoying us as we grow and mature spiritually, in spite of how awkward it looks.

Layla put up such a fight, as I attempted to comb her hair, that I was afraid the neighbors would hear, and call 911. There was no calming her on this day; I even explained to her we were going bye-bye, which usually did the trick. I gave up. I put the comb and brush aside, and laid Layla across my chest. After about ten minutes or so, I thought she had fallen asleep, however she hadn't. She rose up from my chest, reached over, grabbed the brush and handed it to me. I was totally surprised, never-the-less, I just took the brush and began brushing her hair. I did not hear another thing from Layla, until after I finished her hair. At the time of this incident she was fourteen months.

We often do the same when the Lord is grooming and

preparing us for heaven, even when it is for our own good. If a tiny toddler has a conscience and can be convicted, how much more so are we to surrender to the conviction of the Holy Spirit.

As babies do, Layla did fall out of bed. It always happened while she was asleep. After a few of these experiences, she figured out if she got too close to the edge she would fall. At a young age we learn just how far we can go before we fall, even while sleeping we are conscious of that fact. That should be in our Christian walk as well. We need to know the danger signs that lead to sin.

As we develop in our spiritual walk, we become sin conscious, and tend to stay away from dangerous area. Then if and when we give into a sinful temptation, it is after thought and contemplation. Falling and slipping are not the same. On occasion, we will, and do slip, we are not perfect. Thank God for Jesus, provisions have been made.

Today's Challenge

Sing one of your favorite song you learned as a child. Personally mine is, "Yes Jesus loves me". Make sure you listen to the words as you sing. Now here is the challenge sing it 5 times throughout the day. Have fun.

Growing Pains

"When I was a child, I spake as a child, I understood as a child, I thought as a child, but when I became a man I put away childish things" (1st Corinthians 13:11).

"But strong meat belongeth to them that are of full age, even those by reason of use have their senses exercised to discern both good and evil" (Hebrews 5:14).

We will not be stagnant in our spiritual walk, nor will it be dormant. It is called a walk because movement is involved, whether forward or backwards, depending on you. Sometimes I do not feel so good spiritually. I realize those days do come, because we go through seasons, but these particular feelings are different. I will describe them as uncomfortable. During these times I have not deliberately sinned, or done anything displeasing. But on the contrary, I would have received a revelation, a blessing, or experienced the presence of the Lord in an awesome way. After several of these experiences I inquired of the Lord. "Growing Pains". I did not fully understand, but I received, and believed and the understanding came as a result.

In my last year of elementary school, I was one of the big kids, I knew the ropes. I graduated to junior high (middle school) and in that first year, I was timid, shy and insecure. However in the last year of junior high school that feeling of security returned, only to depart upon entering high-school. There is a pattern. And we have that same pattern in our spiritual lives. When we grow spiritually we enter unfamiliar territory which can cause us to feel uncomfortable (Growing Pains).

"As newborn babes, desire the sincere milk of the word that ye may grow thereby" (1st Peter 2:2). To ease those pains we turn to the Word. God is so awesome and so is his Word. All the answers are in the Book.

Today's Challenge

On a calendar begin to note these uncomfortable days, or weeks which ever the case may be. At the end of six months reflect back. Thank God for the growth and the growing pains.

Having Your Heart's Desire

Many people become discouraged; when they feel they are not getting their heart's desire.

"The heart is deceitful above all things and desperately wicked, who can know it? I the Lord search the heart I try the reins, even to give every man according to his ways, and according to the fruit of his doing" (Jeremiah 17:9-10). This may come across as a little harsh, but if you have hatred, envy, strife and other such things in your heart, you desire to have them, you do have a choice. So when you get such things in return, in reality you are getting your hearts desire. The desires must line up, to manifest in our lives. Let's start with our doings, or better yet what we should be doing.

"Delight thyself also in the Lord: and he shall give thee the desires of thine heart" (Psalms 37:4).

According to Webster's delight is: a high degree of pleasure, enjoyment, and joy. We know joy to be a benefit as well as a reward bestowed on children of God. Therefore that scripture is referring to a particular group of people, and these people do specific things.

"Trust in the Lord, and do good, so shalt thou dwell in

the land, and verily thou shalt be fed" (Psalms37:3). Are you on the eligibility list? Not sure? well read on.

"Commit thy way unto the Lord; trust also in him: and he shall bring it to pass. And he shall bring forth thy righteousness as the light, and thy judgement as the noonday" (Psalms 37:5-6). Here these particular people are referred to as possessing righteousness. so let us not be quick in saying we are not getting our heart's desire. God says we can have our desires, and how to obtain them. God is not a man that he should lie.

Today's Challenge

Read and meditate on Psalms 37.

Rejoice and Be Glad

As with all other scripture used in the writing of this book, I referred to the King James Version of the Bible. I do use other versions for study purposes. I found the wording to be different in some scriptures pertaining to today's reading, however in the King James I found constant, and consistent confirmation to clarity what the Lord had given me.

I always thought it to true, that if I rejoiced I was automatically glad. Well, that was my carnal thinking. In order to rejoice and be glad as well is a spiritual principal, as we will see in scripture. "Draw me, we will run after thee; the king hath brought me into his chambers; we will be glad and rejoice in thee, we will remember thy love more than wine: the UPRIGHT love thee" (Song of Solomon 1:4).

"Sing, O daughter of Zion shout, O Israel: be glad and rejoice with all the heart, O daughter of Jerusalem" (Zephaniah 3:14).

"Let us be glad and rejoice, and give honour to him: for the marriage of the Lamb is come, and his wife hath made herself ready"(Revelation 19:7). The last scripture I referred to, plainly shows that we will be in heaven. We know with a certainty who gets to go there, and those are the same ones that are able to rejoice AND be glad.

In order to rejoice AND be glad, one must be a spirit-filled child of God. It is another one of those fringe benefits we have (whew). It is impossible for the two to work in harmony any other way. It is a God Given ability.

In closing I will give these two scenarios of how the world rejoice OR be glad: 1) Someone purchases a new car, shows off and rejoices outwardly, but inwardly worry, what if I become sick and it gets repossessed, what if I wreck it, what if it gets stolen, and so on it goes, he does not have that blessed assurance that all is well. ("The blessing of the Lord, it maketh rich, and he addeth no sorrow to it") (Proverbs 10:22). 2) Someone is sharing good news with a so-called friend, that person rejoices with them outwardly but inwardly wonder why the good fortune did not befall them (envy). Without genuine joy, true gladness does not occur.

Today's Challenge

No matter what the day brings, think about the fact that you are going to heaven when all is said and done. Jesus is coming back to get you. Now rejoice I say AND be glad. We can do that!

Day 29

Loss of a Loved One

I lost my dear mother to cancer when I was fifteen, she was only thirty-six.

"The righteous perisheth, and no man layed it to heart; and merciful men are taken away, none considering that the righteous is taken away from the evil to come" (Isaiah). As I look back over my difficult years, I thank God my mother was not around to see those evil times in my life.

"Precious in the sight of the Lord is the death of his saints" (Psalms 116:15).

It still amazes me how we can turn to the Word of God for any given situation, or tragic event, and find comfort. We serve an amazing God! I hear songs that speak about how He is a father to the fatherless and a mother to the motherless. Although I truly mourned the death of my mother, and longed to have my father be a part of my life, yet I can not help but to say I am blessed. I experienced a type of fullness from God at an early age, that some will never experience. However a lot of others will, if only they accept and receive God in their lives where ever a void may be. It does not necessarily have to be the death of a loved one. It could be a son or daughter going to prison, a broken marriage, disagreement that severs a long time friendship, loss of a job. Whatever area you have this loss in, let the Lord fill that area with his love. And the best part about it is; you will never experience that same loss again. He will never leave us or forsake us.

Today's Challenge

Voluntarily give up a close relationship for 24 hours. Turn off the cell phone completely, if there is an emergency God will handle it, and better than you can at that. Let Him fill that void you will experience today.

Day 30

Be Still and Know that I Am God

"Be still and know that I am God: I will exalted among the heathen, I will be exalted in the earth" (Psalms 46:10)

Throughout this thirty-day journey (longer for some), I have shared many experiences and revelations. My prayer is to be obedient and consistent in my spiritual life, so I can walk worth of my calling. In doing so I know that God will continue to: lead me, guide me, show me, teach me, and keep me, as I be still and know that he is God. AMEN

Today's Challenge

Be still and know that HE is GOD.

About the Author

Deborah Lynne is a woman after God's own heart. What began as a God-given burden for souls became a God-given passion for souls to be saved. Her early childhood dreams of some day writing a book became one and the same with God's perfect will for her life, once she surrendered it to the Lord, with the result being the Anchored Soul. He has truly given her the desire of her heart. She is currently working on her next book entitled "More Anchoring", which will also be a devotional, consisting of weekly readings.If you would like to share how God used this book in your life please e-mail Deborah @ anchoredsouldl@yahoo.com